MORE PAUSE FOR THOUGHT

Also edited by Lavinia Byrne

PAUSE FOR THOUGHT

MORE PAUSE
FOR THOUGHT

✣　✣　✣

Foreword by
TERRY WOGAN

Edited by
LAVINIA BYRNE

Hodder & Stoughton

First published in Great Britain in 2004,
by arrangement with the BBC.

More Pause for Thought is based on the BBC Radio 2 programme.

The BBC logo is a trademark of the British
Broadcasting Corporation and is used
under licence. BBC logo © BBC 1996

Foreword copyright © 2004 by Terry Wogan
Compilation copyright © 2004 by Lavinia Byrne

The right of Lavinia Byrne to be identified as the Compiler of
the Work has been asserted by her in accordance with the
Copyright, Designs and Patents Act 1988.

10 9 8 7 6 5 4 3 2 1

British Library Cataloguing in Publication Data
A record for this book is available from the British Library

ISBN 0 340 86320 X

Printed and bound in Great Britain by Clays Ltd, St Ives, plc

The paper used in this book is a natural recyclable product
made from wood grown in sustainable forests. The hard
coverboard is recycled.

Hodder & Stoughton
A Division of Hodder Headline Ltd
338 Euston Road
London NW1 3BH
www.madaboutbooks.com

FOREWORD

Pause for Thought has been an integral part of *Wake Up to Wogan* since time began. If you're a regular listener, it may seem longer than that, but that's not the fault of the worthies hereinunder. They keep it brief and to the point. I'll take the rap for droning on for aeons, relentlessly pummelling the ears of the unfortunate listener. Just as 'location, location, location' is the call-sign of the wandering estate agent, so 'repetition, repetition, repetition' is the watchword of the daily broadcaster, particularly of an early morning, with the nation still semi-stunned. Of course, predictability and familiarity have their roles to play as well. I am the old carpet in the hall, the peeling wallpaper in the bathroom, the kettle on the hob. People listen, but they're not hanging on my every word. Some may find it mildly amusing, occasionally even the cause of a stifled snigger, but thought-provoking? I think not, your honour.

Which is where *Pause for Thought* comes in. At its best (and trust me, what you've got in this slim volume is the best, the very best) it's a couple of minutes of pure illumination wrestled from a workday, shedding light into the corners of dingy complacency. It's a wake-up call to your attitude, your conscience. The good people whose musings you will read here are not doing it for the money. They're too wise to preach or harangue. All they want is that you sift their words. Try it. Just a couple of minutes at a time, if you like. It may give you pause for thought...

Terry Wogan

There was a Rabbi who was renowned for his brilliance and wisdom and people flocked to seek his advice and council. His scholarship was such that he had the answer to any question, and the solutions he offered to people's problems always worked!

One young man decided to design a question to which – no matter how wise he was – the Rabbi could never get the correct answer. He would hold a butterfly in his fist and ask the Rabbi if it was alive or dead. If the Rabbi said it was dead, he would open his fingers and let it fly away. If he answered that it was alive, then he would gently crush it and open his fingers and prove the Rabbi wrong.

So he went to the Rabbi and asked his question, 'Is it alive or dead?'

The Rabbi peered into the young man's eyes and said, 'The answer to that lies in your hand.'

Rabbi Y.Y. Rubinstein

Conventional living can stifle creativity and leave us feeling dissatisfied. How often do I hear the question: is this really all there is to life? Well the answer is an emphatic NO, but in order to discover that, we have to be prepared to grow old disgracefully, and with an ethic that embraces rather than excludes other people.

Revd Ruth Scott

✛ ✛ ✛

Prayer is about getting to know God. And when that happens, we find that God's concerned with all our needs and longings, the trivial ones as well as the important ones. But we find out at the same time that not everything we want is best for us: not because God's a killjoy but because he wants to move us on from postcards to real pictures, from romance to real love. Within that real love, of course we must ask God for things, and of course he can say No as well as Yes. But we must expect God to have some requests to put to us too. God isn't a bureaucrat who needs endless letters before he'll do anything. Jesus taught us to call him 'Father'.

Rt Revd Tom Wright

Praying can sometimes seem like watching a very dull cricket match. We turn up, we sit or we kneel, we try to concentrate. But nothing seems to happen.

Other people speak of experiences of ecstasy when they pray, of joy or peace, but all we seem to acquire are stiff knees or a numb backside.

In truth, of course, something significant is always happening whenever we turn, as Jesus taught us, as children to the Father who loves us. A relationship of trust is deepening, our perspective is changing. And sticking at it when we seem to get nothing at all from it? That's true prayer, true faith. It really is.

Revd Roy Jenkins

A mother took her six-year-old son Jonathan to a restaurant. Jonathan had been learning prayer in his Religious Class at school so he asked his mum to let him say Grace. As they bowed their heads Jonathan prayed, 'God is great. God is good. Thank you for this food. And I would even thank you more if Mum gets ice-cream by the score. So bless, Lord, this food we eat. Amen.'

Most of the people at nearby tables laughed – except one stern-faced woman who remarked, 'That's what is wrong with this country. Children today don't even know how to pray. Asking God for ice-cream. How awful.'

Jonathan heard the woman and naturally felt very upset and began to cry. He meant no harm with his off-the-cuff prayer. He checked with his mum. 'Is God mad at me now?' he enquired.

His mum hugged him and assured Jonathan that he had done a good job with the prayer and that God was not mad at him. Just then an elderly gentleman came up to their table and assured him: 'Son, that was a beautiful prayer you said.'

'Really?' Jonathan asked.

'Cross my heart,' the man answered. Then in a stage whisper just loud enough for the indignant woman to hear he added, 'Too bad she never asked God for ice-cream. Sometimes a little ice-cream is good for the soul.'

At the end of the meal Mum answered his prayer and ordered ice-cream. Jonathan stared at his ice-cream for a moment and then to his mother's surprise he picked up his dish and carefully brought it over to the woman's table and placed it in front of her. Jonathan politely said, 'Here, this is for you. Ice-cream is good for the soul, and my soul is good enough already.'

Fr Brian D'Arcy

✢ ✢ ✢

The Vedas compare the Lord's blessings to the brilliant rays of the sun. They are always pouring down on us. It is simply up to us to come out of the shadows. And that is exactly what the Vedas exhort: 'Come out of the darkness and into the light.'

That darkness, the Vedas say, is forgetfulness of the Lord and his boundless mercy, and not seeing that his blessings are continuously with us. Of course, we can always pray, but more than anything we need to keep ourselves in the bright light of the Lord's instructions.

Krishna Dharma

✣ ✣ ✣

Fear has a way of clouding the opportunities which present themselves to us; fear often limits our ability to move beyond the place in which the mind is stuck. Remaining in fear prevents us from contributing to and experiencing life in all its fullness.

It has been said that 'courage is fear that has said its prayers'. This may well need to become our reality. We can't do anything as long as we are afraid. It does not mean that we pretend we're not afraid. It means we face our fears head on, not allowing our lives to be dominated by those things we are fearful of. It is only then, with great courage, that we will all be able to strive in doing our best to ensure that we break free from the fears which shackle us.

Revd Rose Hudson-Wilkin

The word 'paradise' is apparently derived from the Persian word for a walled garden. In the Islamic tradition the image of heaven is often presented to us as a beautiful garden with flowing streams and lush verdant foliage, a haven of shade in hot dry world. Islam is very rich in poetry, and many of these poets expressed religious ideas in terms of romantic love and intoxication – not things, I know, that many people would associate with Islam in the west, but there it is.

I think, as a religious individual, that the world around us is full of spiritual power if we are open-minded enough to see it.

Faris Badawi

✤ ✤ ✤

Did you hear about the person who, in an interview, was asked about the last book he'd read? He said it was called the *Concise Oxford Dictionary*, and while he didn't think much of the story he liked the way the author explained what each word meant as he went along.

The last time I went to a school parents'

evening there was a poster on the wall of the English department. It said: 'The limits of my language are the limits of my world.' Meaning: if I don't understand the words, I don't get the message. The tragedy for many people today is that they don't even understand the words relating to the things of God.

Major Charles King

Religious devotion is the process by which we free ourselves from ourselves by directing our concern and love towards others and filling our hearts with God's divine universal and inexhaustible love for creation. Our real and eternal nature is not caught up with all the silly fuss of ego: our real nature sees God's divine beautiful presence in all, like the myriad rays of a single sun, and our hearts are peaceful even when rivers of blood flow, with unbiased love and concern for all. Some call this kind of Islam madness, but it seems to me to be the very basis of sanity.

Faris Badawi

✣ ✣ ✣

Why do individuals of any age turn to stimulants? To drugs, to alcohol, to prescription drugs …? Well, there can be many reasons. But primarily I would suggest that it is to deal with levels of suffering. For many people, life – day-to-day life – is a struggle.

The taking of stimulants is only the symptom of a more fundamental dis-ease. It takes the edge off, it's a momentary escape from one's anxieties and stresses. As any gardener will tell you, you can't kill a weed by lopping off the leaves: you have to remove the root. The root of our country's dependence on stimulants is an underlying dis-ease, and a loss of faith in our own heart's natural capacity for joy, happiness and contentment. This is what we individually and collectively have to tackle if we are to find peace.

Dharmachari Nagaraja

Heaven and hell are not physical places. They are symbolic references to how near or far we are from our Creator. Nearness to God is heaven; and to be far from God is hell.

Baha'u'llah, founder of the Baha'i faith, said it's much simpler than that – we experience nearness to God through service to others.

Fidelma Meehan

✤ ✤ ✤

Paul Theroux tells a story of visiting the camp of an Australian beachcomber. It was full of junk. 'What's it for?' he asked. The old guy told him he was building a raft to sail round Australia. Theroux pointed out that was a big job. 'I'm just doing it slow,' came the reply. 'You can go anywhere in the world if you go slow.'

Revd John Rackley

W e need faith in our nation and it starts by finding faith in ourselves. We all make mistakes – the rich and famous, the poor and homeless, even people of faith. The only person who got it right all the time was Jesus, who met with so many people: the important, the marginalised, the rich and the rejected. His influence and message has built up the faith of millions; and Jesus still does it today.

Commissioner Alex Hughes

A student asked his teacher how he should look for truth. Without answering, the teacher took the pupil to the water's edge and thrust the student's head under the water until he was struggling for breath. Eventually the poor student was pulled out of the water and regained his breath. The teacher then said: 'That's how we must seek the truth. With the urgency of a drowning man who seeks the life-giving air.'

Fidelma Meehan

✥ ✥ ✥

With all this talk about truth being the first casualty of war, I came across a parable which I found helpful.

Once there was a famous Rabbi who had

the annoying habit of always illustrating a truth by telling a story. When asked why he did it, he answered by telling a story.

'There was a time when Truth went around naked,' he began. 'But the people always turned their backs on him. The result was that Truth wandered about the country feeling unwanted and depressed. On his journeys he met Mr Story strolling along, happily dressed in a multi-coloured coat.

' "Truth, why are you so sad?" Story asked.

' "I'm sad because everybody avoids me," Truth replied. "They don't want me."

' "Nonsense," Story insisted, "That's not why people avoid you. Here, borrow my coat and see what happens."

'So Truth put on Story's multi-coloured coat. An extraordinary thing happened. Everywhere he went he was welcomed.

21

'So,' the Rabbi concluded, 'people are not able to face the naked Truth; they much prefer Truth disguised in a story.'

There is a friend of mine who deals in stories and he has this principle about them. He says that all stories are true and some of them actually happened. That really is the value of a story. If we take it literally we get nothing out of it. But if we can see its central truth then the story will help to highlight the truth. A spoonful of sugar helps the medicine go down.

What we sometimes don't realise, though, is that our own lives are stories, and we need to reflect on our stories to discover the Truth behind them. Look carefully at your own life today. Before you go to bed tonight, take time to reflect on the stories of the day. Trust your own story to show you where Truth is.

Fr Brian D'Arcy

✤ ✤ ✤

Hope and struggle are destined to be companions in this life. From such times can emerge all that is best in the human spirit and all that is possible in the life of faith. Those who believe faith is just a prop are missing the point. It's often harder to believe than not to believe. As a friend once said to me: when you can't find the answers, live the questions until they turn into your answers.

Revd John Rackley

✥ ✥ ✥

Religions can never be more than working models because the reality we call God will always be greater than human perception can grasp, and there's no sense in claiming otherwise. Better, as the prophet Micah says, to do justice, love kindness and walk humbly with our God – or at least our imperfect pictures of God. Arrogance and wisdom are mutually exclusive.

Revd Ruth Scott

I slam has a quite temptingly huge literature of religious questioning and Muslims have for hundreds of years tested what we take to be the revealed truths against all sorts of competing ideas. The results of these efforts were often that we changed our notions of what the revelation meant, and realised that our understandings had in fact been deepened. Believing things without testing them to see if they make sense is rather like buying a book and leaving it unopened on a table, and then claiming that we understand what it contains and what it means because we paid for it.

Faris Badawi

✣✣✣

Faith, when it is active, gives us the key to unlock the presence of God in the bits and pieces of our everyday world.

Fr Brian D'Arcy

✣✣✣

W e've all seen proud parents watching over their kids, willing them to do really well. Today each of us should try to live in the memory that God is doing the same.

✣ ✣ ✣

C ynicism is a poor substitute for hope, just as rhetoric is no substitute for truth. Part of our dignity as human beings is a God-given potential to make a difference – if I didn't believe that I wouldn't get up in the morning. But it means not only pressing the 'powers that be' for truth but also living the truth ourselves, for it is truth which sets us free and keeps us free.

Rt Revd Roy Williamson

✣ ✣ ✣

We cannot hide from the uncertainties of life. So in what can we take refuge, where can we find shelter, how can we bear the world? The Buddha taught that the only true refuge is found in our own hearts with the cultivation of understanding, compassion and faith that things may change.

Dharmachari Nagaraja

When the Caliphs asked one of the great legal scholars, more than a thousand years ago, for permission to enforce his legal opinion throughout the empire he said, 'I know what I know. It may be that others, elsewhere, know better than me, so it would be wrong to impose my ideas on others.' He wasn't sure about his own ideas; however, he had great faith in the ability of others to think at least as well as himself. That is the thing: religious doubt is directed towards ourselves, not others.

Otherwise we can't develop, because not to doubt yourself leaves no room for change, and the Prophet said, 'If you don't make some progress, every day, you're losing out.'

And we can't change unless we doubt ourselves, doubt that our present condition is good enough. You can have faith in doubt, so that it's not painful or destabilising. We doubt that there is anything on earth that it's worth doing wrong to obtain. Our faith makes our doubt an effective protection for others from our intolerant or ignorant assumptions; it is a source of happiness. Well, I think it may be – God alone knows.

Faris Badawi

✢ ✢ ✢

God is not a celestial regulator making sure everything works according to routine. He's rather like an inventor letting new ways and opportunities emerge unexpectedly.

And if that's the case, then faith is a useful way of life. Faith doesn't depend on everything being the same or always working perfectly, but rather is prepared to believe that there is a meaning in what happens even when it isn't obvious. Faith helps us cope with the messiness of life.

It accepts the surprises of life, both the pleasant and the unpleasant. It doesn't need the security of everything being just as we want it to be. It accepts there's more going on than we know or hope to understand. George MacLeod, the founder of the Iona Community, used to say about an unexpected surprise: if you think that's a coincidence then may you live a dull life. He believed that a life with faith in God was one that never runs out of possibilities.

Revd John Rackley

✣ ✣ ✣

Imagine a society without trust where cynicism ruled the day and none of us knew who to fall back on. A world in which everyone was guilty of guile, until proven innocent or naive.

So in our imperfections we all need a trustworthy fallback position. A platform of values on which to build tough and trusting relationships strong enough to endure our temporary failures.

The values which prompt and fuel our trustworthiness simply have to come from beyond ourselves. As a Christian, it's the ability to trust God which gives me my final fallback position.

As the psalmist puts it, trust in the Lord with all your heart and don't lean on your own understanding. We need to trust God, not because we're stupid but because we're fallible.

Trust in public or private life is a gift of God. For ultimately we only value people we can really trust.

Revd Joel Edwards

Well, I was taught as a child that if you can't say anything good about a person, you shouldn't say anything at all. I'm also aware that when you point a finger at someone, your other three fingers point back at you. And none of us is perfect. Jesus said that when someone is accused of wrongdoing, the first stone should be cast by 'he who is without sin' – and not many of us fall into that category. For Jesus, hypocrisy was pretty well the greatest sin. He was willing to forgive most wrongdoing, but he couldn't abide hypocrites. 'Whitewashed sepulchres', he called them.

Now, I'm a Christian, and that means hypocrisy is a constant danger. Christianity sets such high standards that failure, to one degree or another, is inevitable. But I read a great quote this week: 'The hypocrite pretends to be something he is not in order to make a good impression. The Christian strives to be something he is not, in order eventually to become it.'

Major Charles King

At the Seattle Special Olympics, nine contestants, all physically or mentally disabled, assembled at the starting line of what was to be the 100-yards contest.

At the gun they all started out, not exactly in a dash but with a relish to run the race to the best of their ability and hopefully finish and win. All, that is, except one little boy who stumbled on the track, tumbled over a few times and began to cry out of sheer fright.

The other eight heard the boy cry. They slowed down and looked back.

Then they all turned around and went back … every single one of them.

One little girl with Down's Syndrome bent down and kissed him and said, 'This will make it better.'

Then all nine linked arms and walked together to the finishing line. Everyone in the stadium stood and the cheering went on for minutes.

People who were there are still telling the story. Why?

Because deep down we know this one thing: what really matters in this life is helping others win, even if it means slowing down and changing course ourselves.

As the saying goes: 'A candle loses nothing by lighting another candle from itself.'

People we call handicapped are the people who teach us this truth best.

Fr Brian D'Arcy

✤ ✤ ✤

To have hope is to have a wonderful gift. It believes that events will turn out right. It is not burdened by the need to force the issue. It does not get downcast but waits for the moment when hope blossoms into fact.

Revd John Rackley

✤ ✤ ✤

It seems to me that when we get things wrong, as if life just seems like a daily struggle to survive, then I have to believe that God is there, that he is in the mess, but that ultimately 'all will be well'. I have to believe that my God is a God of hope.

Fr Shaun Middleton

✢ ✢ ✢

Let's look for godly interruptions in our daily lives and expect the unexpected.

Revd Rob Gillion

✢ ✢ ✢

After thirty-six years of priesthood I still do not know what to say to someone who is dying of a terminal illness, to a parent whose son or daughter has tragically died. To someone suffering a black depression, to someone plumbing the depths of grief because of a broken relationship. And perhaps it's better that I haven't found the right words because words so often are a smokescreen, a way of avoiding the pain, the reality. Better than words is to be there – watching and waiting. Like the women who waited at the cross and at the tomb. Women are better at staying with someone in their pain. Men often run away, as the disciples did. Good Friday unites us all. We share in the suffering of so many who are waiting at a cross or a tomb or a hospital today. Iraq is the newest and latest of so many terrible tragedies.

The cry of pain that rises to God from this tortured earth – the victims of war and terror, starving children, the homeless – IS the cry of the cross.

Christ on the Cross is the cry of humanity to God. God hears that cry.

Revd Murray Grant

✤ ✤ ✤

Someone once described the difference between a pessimist and an optimist as being this. A pessimist wakes up and stumbles out of bed, opens the curtains and says, 'Good God, morning?' The optimist bounds out of bed, runs to the window, throws open the curtains and exclaims, 'Good morning, God.'

Given the choice between these two, I prefer to live my life as an optimist, as one who views the glass as being half-full, as one who sees possibilities rather than problems, as a person of faith who looks at the future with hope rather than despair. I'd rather live with a thankful heart than with complaining lips.

Revd Dr Stephen C. Rettenmayer

Coming here on the train and the tube I have been alongside scores of people but there has been no communication. It's not done to smile, and eye contact could be seen as invasive. It is sad that we feel a smile could be misinterpreted and we worry about all the possible boundaries that we might accidentally cross. Somehow the balance has been lost. No, we don't want intrusion, but sometimes a human response would make it all less grim, less serious and less lonely.

Fr Wilfrid McGreal

As I travel around in my locality, I see very little evidence of self-confidence. I have committed myself to do all that I can to encourage and nurture a sense of self-confidence in the young people around me. Sadly for many, they have behind them a history of abuse, injustice and oppression. We spend our time listening to negative voices; we buy and listen to music that denigrates our common humanity; we consciously or unconsciously feed in a frenzied way on the things that contribute to our lack of confidence.

The challenge for each of us is to cultivate that self-confidence. I do that by not believing the negative 'stuff' that is out there; I do that by believing and embracing all that is good in life; I cultivate confidence by seeking the best in my fellow human beings. The thing that disadvantages us is not what other people do to us, believe or say about us. The thing that disadvantages us the most is our lack of self-confidence.

My journey of self-confidence begins with the belief that God has created me for something good.

Revd Rose Hudson-Wilkin

If it's someone new at work or new to the neighbourhood and they aren't doing things quite the way they should, with just a smile and a bit of encouragement they'll soon learn to fit in just fine.

Rabbi Y.Y. Rubinstein

✤ ✤ ✤

Sometimes we miss a cry for help from an individual who disguises it – in difficult behaviour, for example, or reclusiveness, or simply by putting on a bold front when inside they're breaking their heart. We need to be perceptive to the needs of others, and we can't be that if we're thinking only of ourselves. Jesus told a relevant story. We know it as the Parable of the Good Samaritan.

Major Charles King

✤ ✤ ✤

It is said that love is blind, but friendships are clairvoyant. A true friend is someone who reaches for your hand and finds your heart. They allow us to work as if we don't need the money, love as if we have never been hurt and dance as if no one is watching.

Fr Brian D'Arcy

✤ ✤ ✤

I have always appreciated the fact that Jesus commanded us to love ourselves as well as to love God and our neighbours. In a world full of moral ugliness and injustices, we need to be embraced by beauty for us to be healthy and whole human beings. So go ahead and treat yourself! Whether it is listening to a symphony or another kind of music, watching a rainbow or being mesmerised by a sunset, walking through a garden or visiting an art museum, smelling roses or enjoying the smile of a baby, indulge yourself! Beauty is God's gift to us. In the midst of your busy life, make time for it, and then tell the Giver of all good gifts and beauty 'thank you'.

Revd Dr Stephen C. Rettenmayer

✤ ✤ ✤

Three sons – Tom, Dick and Harry – left home, went into business and prospered. They discussed what they had bought their mother for Mother's Day. The first said, 'I've bought a huge mansion for her to live in.' The second said, 'I've given her a luxury limousine, complete with chauffeur.' The third said, 'You know how much Mama enjoys reading the Bible. But she can't see very well these days so I've sent her a remarkable parrot which can recite the entire Bible. It took its previous owner twelve years to teach it. Now all Mama has to do is name a chapter and verse, and the parrot will recite it.'

Soon after that conversation, their mother sent out her letters of thanks. 'Thomas,' she said, 'the house you gave me is so huge. I only live in one room but I have to clean the whole house. Richard, I'm too old to travel. I'll hardly ever use the car. But Harold, the little chicken you sent was delicious!'

Major Charles King

We all share a desire for happiness. Nobody wants to be a loser, and when we are touched by success or happiness it is only natural that we grasp at it – we want it to stay, we don't want to suffer its passing. And yet it is this constant grasping after happiness, a constant sense of dissatisfaction, that drives us on. We seem to find it almost impossible to be content with what we have. Happiness, the Buddha taught, arises when one realises the truth that good health is one's greatest possession; that contentment is the greatest of riches; that trust is the finest of relationships; and that freedom and liberty are the highest bliss.

Dharmachari Nagaraja

Over the years my job has made me a student of human nature and convinced me that happiness is the thing that people desire most. It wasn't a theologian but a comedian, Ken Dodd, who put it so well when he sang 'Happiness – the greatest gift that I possess.'

In other words, though external circumstances may play a part, the secret of lasting happiness lies within ourselves and our inner resources. It was St Paul who said, 'I have learnt to be content whatever the circumstances.'

'You must be joking!' some might say. But no, he was deadly serious and spoke from experience. He'd been an unhappy, discontented person until faith became part of his inner resources. Then he seemed able to cope with anything life threw at him.

We might think that's beyond us, but most of us have been surprised by our own inner strength when the going gets tough and so, with the addition of a little faith and the help of good friends, perhaps, lasting happiness is within reach of us all.

Rt Revd Roy Williamson.

✣ ✣ ✣

There really isn't any point in trying to cut yourself off from ordinary life and people in the hope that then you can be truly religious. Funnily enough, I've found that real life and real religion are pretty much the same thing. All the themes of religious behaviour are concerned with quite ordinary things like kindness, openness, intelligence – the things ordinary people exhibit every day.

Faris Badawi

✣ ✣ ✣

When the New Testament says, 'Each of you should look not only to your own interests but also to the interests of others,' it has in mind a healthy kind of compromise which all human relationships need in order to survive. It could mean that as you roll out of bed to set out for the day, you might have to give way to someone else in order to make the relationship better than it was yesterday.

Revd Joel Edwards

✣ ✣ ✣

We're not designed to be self-sufficient. From the moment of conception we are in relationship. Our relationships help us discover who we are. That's why some of us instinctively wonder what's going on when medical science suggests that a child can be made from the eggs of an unborn foetus. We're not being reactionary. But we're saying: how can such a creature be a human being? We need more than ourselves to fulfil our potential. We need origins, heroes, role-models, saviours and gods.

There's more to naming a child than a party for friends and family. It's providing her with horizons and discoveries that help her discover more about herself. It's offering a source of restoration and completion beyond herself when times get confusing, as Paul found in Christ.

Revd John Rackley

Basically, the Highway Code is about relationships: how to keep ourselves and other road users safe and happy. Unfortunately, it has a limited scope and doesn't help us in our relationships off the road – relationships at home, work and everywhere else.

For this kind of guidance, a Spiritual Highway Code is needed, which has been provided by the world's religions.

Today, many people have become so disillusioned with religion that they have totally discarded the Spiritual Highway Code it offers. But, since the vacuum left by religion isn't filled, we still have this yearning to find something, a faith or belief, that gives purpose and meaning in life. So, to fill up the vacuum, we may decide to make up our own Spiritual Highway Codes and give up on religion altogether. But before we throw out the baby with the bathwater, Baha'u'llah has an explanation as to why religion is in decline.

Religion is like a lamp that, down through the centuries, has been obscured by layer upon layer of prejudice, interpretation and dogma. The result is darkness, which is where we are today. But there's hope.

Every time religion has gone into decline in the past, a new lamp has been lit and a new religion has been born. Its teachings then became the new Spiritual Highway Code.

Fidelma Meehan

Maybe real peacemaking begins when I first address my own capacity to hurt others. Perhaps if I did that I wouldn't need to find scapegoats for personal unresolved issues. I need to use my anger, not to destroy but to work for justice, to create heaven on earth, not hell.

It's said that a bad-tempered samurai once commanded a Zen master to explain the concept of heaven and hell. The monk replied scornfully, 'You think I'm going to waste my time explaining things to an ignorant oaf like you?' Hearing this the samurai flew into a rage and, unsheathing his sword, yelled, 'I shall kill you for your rudeness.'

'That,' replied the monk calmly, 'is hell.'

Stunned by the truth the master had pointed out about the fury gripping him, the samurai calmed down, sheathed his sword and, bowing deeply, thanked the monk for his insight.

'And that,' responded the monk, 'is heaven.'

Revd Ruth Scott

✢ ✢ ✢

Our basic mistake is to think of happiness and security as something that comes from outside: if we get what we want or organise our lives in a way that we find pleasing then we will be happy, and when things don't work out – as they never do – we become frustrated and depressed. Happiness never lasts when it's based on controlling the world and others, because we change and the world changes and there is nothing we can do about it.

Once, the great Mulla Nasruddin stole an ox, killed it and skinned it. He was making his getaway when the owner discovered his butchered animal and began wailing. 'Strange case of cause and effect,' thought Nasruddin. 'I kill the ox and the owner sounds as if he's being skinned!'

Muslims like me, who find ourselves a bit at the sharp end at the moment, have a source of happiness that is the heart of all spiritual paths – a commitment to kindness, charity and love. Whatever our circumstances, it is more dependable as a source of joy than a beautiful partner or a great life or even a huge unchallengeable army.

Faris Badawi

✢ ✢ ✢

Real wealth, which is inexhaustible and nothing to do with the bank balance, is a richness of heart and generosity of spirit.

Dharmachari Nagaraja

✦ ✦ ✦

I think real maturity is neither total self-sufficiency nor total dependence. To be grown up is to be interdependent. You've come of age when you're big enough to admit that you need other people to complement you as you are.

It's what it means to be human.

And from a God's-eye view of independence, being human means that we recognise our dependence on him. It's not so much that God has to direct every detail of what we do every day. But it does matter to him that we recognise just how much our humanity is tied in to his very existence.

'In him we live and move and have our being.' Our lives are bound up in who he is, because we are made in the image of God.

If God is dead we are forever entombed.

Individual effort and solo flights have their place. But we are at our very best not in those moments of fierce successful solitude – our spiritual health comes when we find others with whom we can connect, and with the God in whose image we are made.

It reminds me of the thirty-something businessman I met some years ago. His ambition was to earn his first million by the time he was thirty. And he did it. The only problem was that he sacrificed people for profits. He made his million. But he had no one with whom to share it.

Living with God in community is ultimate independence. Because freedom always feels better with other people.

Revd Joel Edwards

✠ ✠ ✠

People today are very worried about weapons of mass destruction: we are looking for them everywhere. But there is one weapon of mass destruction that is hiding in plain sight. It is present in every country. It's invisible, odourless and easy to transport, but it's not undetectable.

Hypocrisy – the misapplication of moral principles, holding others to standards that we do not accept for ourselves. It's an attitude that is almost the apogee of destructiveness. It has no equal. Hypocrisy lays waste all around us, wrecking relationships and causing unhappiness and insecurity.

Faris Badawi

A ccepting ourselves is a necessary condition to accepting others and being accepted by others, including God. In other words, if I am to believe that God can love me and that other people can accept me as well, then I have to be friends with myself the way I was. The way I was may be an embarrassment to me now, but it seemed the right thing to do at the time, and that person shouldn't be a stranger to me, but a friend I'm happy to meet again occasionally.

Rt Revd Kieran Conry

There's a lovely story in the Jewish Talmud. Two schools, founded by two older contemporaries of Jesus called Hillel and Shammai, were arguing about a matter of Jewish law, and both felt they were right. Eventually a heavenly voice declared that both views were the words of the living God, but because a definite ruling was required, the way of the school of Hillel would be followed. Why? Because the members of that school were kind and modest, they studied both sides of the argument, mentioned the school of Shammai before their own school and didn't actively seek greatness, or the power to impose that goes with it. They weren't anxious to win at all costs. These virtues, said the heavenly voice, deserved the highest reward. And wouldn't such attitudes make a difference to many of our conflicts today?

Revd Ruth Scott

✣ ✣ ✣

Guru Nanak, direct as ever, taught that a live lived is a life wasted if we live it without giving some 'added value' to the lives of those around us and to the lives of those that follow. He reminded us that putting a little back adds to the fullness and enjoyment of our own life.

Indarjit Singh

✣ ✣ ✣

Even though there is a Jewish teaching that says you should keep away from a bad neighbour, you can often turn a bad neighbour into a good one by offering them a bit of friendship, a bit of kindness and an invitation for a meal.

Rabbi Y.Y. Rubinstein

✛ ✛ ✛

I heard last week of a drive-through restaurant somewhere in the USA where a customer, when paying for her order, told the cashier to take enough money to pay for coffee for the person in the car behind her – a complete stranger.

That customer was so surprised and pleased that he did the same. He paid for coffee for the person behind him. And do you know, it continued like that down the queue, until in the end twenty-seven people paid for the coffee of the person behind them.

Major Charles King

✣ ✣ ✣

Did you know that the average five-year-old laughs about 150 times a day, while the average forty-five-year-old laughs eight times a day? What does that say? As we grow older, we tend to take the world and ourselves too seriously! 'But the world is a scary place,' you say, 'and we need to take its problems seriously!' I would agree. But if we take them too seriously, if we become so caught up in those problems that we can't see anything else but them, we lose perspective and objectivity. Laughter can help us keep a healthy perspective on life.

Revd Dr Stephen C. Rettenmayer

✤ ✤ ✤

In church on Sunday we were still celebrating Easter. One of the children thrust a large piece of paper into my hand. On it was a picture of a rock with a big hole in it, and a figure. A picture of the empty tomb.

'But who's that?' I asked.

'My gran,' I was told.

'I didn't realise she was there when Jesus rose,' I said.

'Don't be silly!' said my young friend. 'But I think she's got an Easter face.'

And I know what she means. The person she's describing has had an extraordinary life. She's known her full share of tragedy and setback but has never let them overwhelm her. It shows not only in her face but in the way in which she takes on life. She's told me that she expects each day to contain a surprise, and she doesn't mind whether it's comfortable or not. She's learnt to cope with fear.

I've been told that all it takes for something new to begin is when a few people are not frightened of being insecure – I call that Easter spirit.

Revd John Rackley

There are some images which are almost impossible to erase from our minds. For example, who can ever forget the famous picture of a nine-year-old girl, naked, screaming in terror from burns as she ran from a napalm attack during the Vietnam War. Her name was Kim Phuc. And that picture turned American public opinion against the Vietnam War and changed Kim's life for ever.

Now, thirty years later, Kim travels the world on a Christian Forgiveness Campaign. And she uses the picture to remind us of the evils of war.

In London recently she explained why she does it. 'I am a victim of war,' she says. 'I came from war and I know the value of peace. My wish and my dream is that everybody around the world should respect peace. Let them know that war destroys, kills and causes loss. Nobody wins. From my point of view I don't want another victim to suffer like me.'

Mrs Kim is adamant that she is not a politician. She is more concerned to give the view of a child who, at nine years of age, learnt about war when four napalm bombs were dropped on her village north of Saigon in a botched US raid.

Her burns were so severe that she was given little chance of survival. In fact her recuperation took almost ten years. Then, later in life, she began to study medicine. The Vietnamese government realised her propaganda value and took her out of medical school to campaign against the evils of capitalism.

Kim realised she was becoming the victim

all over again. And so she defected to Canada in 1992.

But a reporter outed her there, too. She realised that trying to escape the picture was futile. So she decided to use it to promote peace. She set up a charity to help children injured by war. By now she has been able to forgive the pilot who dropped the bombs and is a Goodwill Ambassador for UNESCO.

She and her husband have two sons; one is the same age as she was when her life was destroyed by war. And so she says, 'When people see that picture they can see in my face and in my brother's face how terrified, how scared we are and how horrible war can be. We did not do anything wrong, so why did we have to suffer like this?'

This morning, when the whole world seems to be hell-bent on war again, that's an extremely good question. Why is it that it is always the innocent who suffer most in war?

Fr Brian D'Arcy

✛ ✛ ✛

And we should know better. Our generation is the first ever to have had an objective view of our world: those first pictures of planet Earth taken from space. That round, shimmering, blue and green, fragile-looking globe spinning in the darkness of space. And it truly is bright and beautiful. Given to us, to supply all our needs, by God. Who told us in the Bible that we have to care for it. To share it equally and to look after it.

Thank God for all the environmentalists who have alerted us to the dangers of what we are doing to this, our one and only earthly home. It's all and everything we've got.

We can't afford to mess it up.

And how shall we answer to God if we have to admit to ruining his masterpiece of creation?

Revd Murray Grant

Peace seems a million miles away. But as someone has said, a journey of a million miles begins with a single step. However, even a single step is impossible when you're stubbornly standing your ground. Ironically, the secret of world peace probably lies in the Middle East, just as it did two thousand years ago.

Major Charles King

If religious leaders and dogmatists were to focus more on the inequalities that rob so many millions of their human dignity, I am sure religion would cease to be a source of conflict and become more of a unifying presence.

Oliver McTernan

When the last Gulf War broke out I was in El Salvador, where there was a civil war raging. In a garrison town in the hills I met an Irish nun whose small convent was used as a refuge by men who'd been tortured at the military barracks. She showed me a thick file with copies of reports she'd sent out of the country. When soldiers had raided the house, she survived only because she'd buried that file in the garden, with just minutes to spare.

'But aren't you frightened?' I asked her. She looked me straight in the eye.

'I'm scared witless most of the time,' she said.

But she didn't let that fear stop her. She knew that God had called her to stand by these desperately poor and persecuted people. And scared as she was, she was staying.

Revd Roy Jenkins

✜ ✜ ✜

A peaceful world is made up of peaceful people. Each of us can therefore contribute to world peace by becoming peaceful ourselves. The ancient Sanskrit text, the Bhagavad-Gita, explains that three things are required to achieve peace.

First, we should always be conscious of the Supreme Lord, recognising that all our endeavours should aim to please him. Second, we should see that he is the true proprietor of everything. And finally, we should see that he is our dearest friend. A person in this frame of mind is always peaceful.

Krishna Dharma

I was back home in Northern Ireland recently and heard that Belfast is hoping to become the City of Culture in 2008. The only problem is the city's twenty-six giant walls, one of which is known as the Peace Wall. You'd think with a name like that, the Peace Wall would be an advantage to a city – until you realise it was built to keep people from killing each other.

Imagine how bad this looks for a City of Culture bid! In one of his routines, Billy Connelly talked about a cemetery in Northern Ireland where even the dead Catholics were separated from the dead Protestants by an underground brick wall. We laughed – until I realised it was true!

Now, thirty years after the walls were built, Belfast's bid for City of Culture means that the walls will either be torn down or turned into local attractions by being painted and covered in fabrics.

But no matter how you dress them up, the real dividing walls, the walls of hatred in the hearts and minds of people, will never look good. These, like the cement walls, have to be destroyed.

Fidelma Meehan

Yesterday, after waiting twenty-two years for planning permission and apparently in the face of widespread opposition, Spanish Muslims opened a newly built mosque in the ancient city of Granada. A thousand years ago, when many parts of Europe were still pretty uncivilised, this region of Spain, which was then under Muslim rule, was renowned for both learning and tolerance. Muslims, Jews and Christians worked closely together in developing a civilisation and culture that was described at the time by a German nun as 'the brilliant ornament of the world'. Sadly, the nuns who live next door to the newly opened mosque in Granada today do not share the same sense of openness to their Muslim neighbours, for according to press reports they have not only built their boundary wall higher but have crowned it with broken glass. I have picked up on this story as I fear that image of higher boundary walls symbolises far too often the relationships that exist today between the different faith groups in the world. I know that there are those who work hard to promote better understanding and co-operation between the different religions, but in general, for whatever reason, believers seem to prefer to work in opposition to one another rather than in harmony. Until those who profess belief come not only to recognise but also to actively promote the right of others to believe and to act differently, I fear religion will continue to be more a source of conflict than a source of reconciliation in our world.

Oliver McTernan

Several of the emails read out on some of the TV programmes during the last few weeks are already beginning to speak about the safety of 'our boys' and our desire to see them back home safely. The newspapers, too, through their headlines and pictures tell a similar story.

But who are 'our boys'? In the midst of any crisis such as we face today, we stand in danger of failing to recognise the common humanity which we share, and it is this failure that allows us to dehumanise each other. We forget that mothers all over the world weep inconsolably at the death of their children. We forget that children all over the world will cry themselves to sleep for the fathers brutally taken from them and whom they will never see. We forget that lovers all over the world are devastated that the man or woman in their lives will no longer share their dreams, their hopes or their beds. We forget that the tears of every man, woman or child, irrespective of creed or culture, cry out with the same pain and anguish.

Revd Rose Hudson-Wilkin

What a different society we would live in if everyone with power and influence – politicians, civil service mandarins, bosses, trade union leaders, celebrities – saw themselves as servants instead of tsars or stars. I don't mind them being well rewarded for their talent, but people who put a lot of effort into looking good should remember that arrogance is very unattractive. I'm also sad when people miss out on another great truth Jesus taught: that it's better to give than to receive, better to minister than to be ministered unto. That's why God chose first the stable and then the cross.

Humility and the willingness to serve others seem not to be highly regarded by those who award this world's prizes. But if the gospel is true, it's the meek who will inherit the earth, and they're the ones who really can die laughing.

Major Charles King

✢ ✢ ✢

You know, we've got more than our fair share of social problems. But the one question we're not supposed to ask is: why? Instead, it's fashionable to look at such problems from the wrong end. Let me give a few examples.

We have Europe's highest rate of teenage pregnancies. Solution? Issue more and more condoms to ever-younger children.

We have a growing drugs problem, particularly among the young. Solution? Decriminalise drugs and make them more freely available.

We have a growing problem of alcohol

abuse. Solution? Deregulate drinking hours and make alcohol more freely available. Result? An even more alarming increase in alcohol abuse and related crime.

Not surprisingly, these attitudes have led to an increase in ever more violent crime. A report last week reminded us that our prison population had risen over the last ten years from a little over 40,000 to more than 70,000!

The problem is that all our shin-pads solutions only make things worse. I know it's desperately unfashionable and not in line with the mood of the times to say this, but what about giving the other three Rs – right, wrong and responsibility – a try?

Indarjit Singh

A very affluent father decided that he needed to expose his son to the way less prosperous people lived. So Dad took Junior on a trip to the countryside where he had arranged for them to stay on a farm for a few days with a family far less affluent than they were. Upon returning home, the father asked his son what he had learnt on their trip to the country and their stay with a poor family.

The son replied, 'I saw that we have one dog, but they have four. We have a pool that reaches to the middle of our garden, but they have a creek that has no end. We have imported lanterns in our garden, but they have the stars at night. Our patio reaches to the front yard, but they have the whole horizon. We have a small piece of land to live on, but they have fields that go beyond our sight. We have servants who serve us, but they serve one another and others. We buy our food, but they grow theirs. We have walls around our property to protect us, but they have friends to protect them.'

The father was speechless. Then the son added, 'It showed me how "poor" we are!'

Revd Dr Stephen C. Rettenmayer

All the newspapers and news bulletins these days are full of discussion about whether Iraq had weapons of mass destruction. It's part of the classic question: how can an all-powerful, all-loving God allow bad things to happen?

The best answer I can come up with is 'because he wants us to take responsibility for our lives', which means giving us free will, with all the possibilities that entails of us getting it wrong. Which we do, with painful regularity. He could have created a perfect world and not allowed us to spoil it, but we would all have been robots, with no minds of our own.

Belief in God is based not on knowledge but on faith and trust. I believe in God because I have decided to, not because I have irrefutable evidence. And having decided to believe without the benefit of proof, I'm prepared to accept not knowing the answers to some important questions. Trusting without knowing for sure is what faith is all about.

Major Charles King

✤ ✤ ✤

I have at home a small metal cross from Liberia. It was made by a man who lost his father, two brothers and two sisters in the war. It's rough and battered, which seems quite appropriate for an instrument of execution, all the more so because it's been shaped from a cartridge left behind after the fighting – a sign of peace from a symbol of death.

It's a sign of God's mercy, too. As I looked at it yesterday, I thought: that's a reminder we always need, and especially if we feel we've been forced unfairly to take the blame for others, made the whipping boy. One sacrificial lamb is enough to guarantee the love of the only person whose verdict ultimately matters.

Revd Roy Jenkins

The world seems to be having its share of human tragedy lately. For those sadly involved, the question 'why me?' is so often asked. As I'm sure you know, Hinduism includes the doctrine of karma. But to many that seems like an insensitive answer that simply adds guilt to the pain already felt. 'It's your own fault, your karma.'

But karma is not about blame: it is about taking responsibility for our acts and accepting the natural consequences. Surely this is the way we all want to live, free to act as we please and to get the results. But some of those results are not what we expect or want. Although we always aim for happiness, sometimes we suffer.

In my efforts to train my children I teach them that they have choices, but each choice is accompanied by a certain consequence. I want them to learn which choices lead to their happiness, and which don't. Obviously, as their father I love them deeply and want only what is best for them. But, as we all know, children are not naturally attracted to the best things – they require training.

The Bhagavad-Gita tells us that God is also training us, his children. The do's and don'ts of scripture are directions meant for our happiness. The Lord is not a killjoy, but is simply steering us away from things he knows will end in pain, just as the loving parent does with his child. But if we choose to ignore him, then we choose the painful consequence. To my endless frustration, I find my children choosing the pain of chores and lost privileges many times before they learn. It seems we too often make the wrong choices – I know I am always doing it. But gradually I am learning. By choosing the Lord's directions, as difficult as they may seem in the beginning, I am realising that the results are always good.

In accepting responsibility for my situation I feel empowered and a sense of relief rather than guilt. Sure, I make mistakes, but that's part of the learning process. And although the pain is sometimes hard to bear, I always know that the person in control loves me and wants only one thing, my ultimate happiness.

Krishna Dharma

There has been so much in the news to do with change, with as many people voting for the changes as those voting against. Throughout, we seem to cling to the illusion that our lives will always be the same, or of how wonderful things were in the good old days – certainly with the longing almost that things could go back to the way they were. We often take it quite personally if there are changes which we believe threaten our way of life.

During this Easter season we have been following the way things changed dramatically for the disciples. The change happened so fast that they struggled to even recognise the resurrected Christ in their midst – after all, he did not look the same, it was not what they were used to. There were even those who insisted that they would not believe unless they saw with their own eyes and touched with their own hands.

For us to find fulfilment in our journeys throughout life, we must be willing to embrace change. Our lives are not meant to be lived in a straight line, nor are they handed to us whole. It is through the changes of life that we must learn to put the pieces together in a way that is creative, in a way that shows our ability to grow and become.

It is our willingness to change that allows us to embrace the unknown.

Revd Rose Hudson-Wilkin

The Buddha taught that it is futile to try to grasp hold of pleasure. Our joys, our happiness – they are all so transitory. But in the same way so are our pains, our sorrows, our suffering. If we can open to that, everything can change; and if we live that truth deeply enough, we can know true happiness.

Dharmachari Nagaraja

✢ ✢ ✢

When we stop changing it is only because we have stopped living, and living is our primary duty for the days we have allotted to us. A religious mystic was once asked to advise a chronically bad-tempered person who was always angry and horrible to everyone all the time. He went and knocked on his door and the angry man opened it. The mystic stuck his fist in the man's face and asked him, 'What would you call this?'

'A fist,' the man replied.

'And if it was always like this,' the mystic asked, 'what would you call it?'

'Deformed,' the man replied.

So let's move with the times and use all that we have learnt in the past to improve the future. Because it's coming, whatever we may say, and shaking our fists at it won't change a thing.

Faris Badawi

✦ ✦ ✦

Yesterday I cancelled my membership of the motoring organisation I've belonged to since I started driving at the age of seventeen. They're excellent, and have rescued me when I've broken down on more occasions than I care to remember – but they're just too expensive these days. You can get the same cover elsewhere for much less.

But it was jolly hard to cancel. The girl I spoke to on the phone just wouldn't give up on me. She kept offering me better discounts, but she still couldn't get anywhere near the price I'd been offered elsewhere.

In the end she made one last effort. 'It will be an awful wrench for you,' she said, 'leaving us after thirty-six years.'

For goodness sake, they're a motoring organisation! It's not as though I was dumping my grandmother in a lay-by on Dartmoor and driving off!

'A wrench?' I said. 'I don't know about that. It's not as though you send me a Christmas card or anything!'

'I'm sure we can manage a Christmas card if that's what you want,' she said.

Full marks to her for trying. If the churches tried as hard not to lose members, many congregations would be a lot bigger.

At the end of the day, though, they couldn't keep me as – even after thirty-six years – I have no relationship with them. I give them money once a year, and they rescue me when I get into difficulties. But we don't love each other. We go months and months without even speaking!

Some people's relationship with God is like that. They do nothing to nurture it. They never go to his house. Never speak to him. But, despite that, they like to feel he'll be there for them if they ever need help.

Well, the good news is, he will. Just as I'll always turn out in the middle of the night to go and help my children if they ever need me. But I wouldn't like that to be the extent of my relationship with them. I want to share the good times too.

And I'm sure our Father in heaven feels much the same.

Major Charles King

In reality people approach life from very different places and with different temperaments, histories, hopes and expectations. No wonder we see things differently. What's needed isn't condemnation but constructive conversation and careful listening. In a diverse world we all need time to adjust our focus to see through the eyes of other people who may also be wondering why we can't see what's so obvious to them.

Revd Ruth Scott

✢ ✢ ✢

You and I may not be able to change yesterday with all its atrocities, but we can ensure that we have a hand in creating our tomorrow. There is a wonderful Chinese proverb which says: 'If there is light in the soul, there will be beauty in the person. If there is beauty in the person, there will be harmony in the house. If there is harmony in the house, there will be order in the nation. If there is order in the nation, there will be peace in the world.'

The religious song was correct, after all, when it said, 'Let there be peace on earth, and let it begin with me.' We change the despair and hopelessness around us by ensuring that the light in our souls is burning brightly – creating beauty, harmony, order and peace.

Revd Rose Hudson-Wilkin

How you see and experience others is the bread and butter, meat and drink of the religious life. When I lived in Ireland I spent three days fishing with the late Paul Deasy – God rest his soul – in Bantry Bay. We spent three days catching whiting, but the net always contained some strange denizen of the deep, and as I gingerly shovelled the weird creature into a creel I would ask Paul what it was. Well, the first one, he told me, was nothing but an old herringhog.

A little later an obviously quite different but no less unknown fish was also a herringhog, and so it went on till there were seven or eight very different little monsters gathered in the box. All were, I had it on Mr Deasy's authority, herringhogs. Paul was no fool, and really it made a lot of sense. A herringhog was a fish that was none of Mr Deasy's business, and they were all the same in that way, hence they all belonged to the extensive genus herringhog. I'm quite sure if I'd come up in the nets I would have ended up in the bait box with the other herringhogs.

In the same manner there is a beautiful slogan used by the Muslim Sufis in dealing with others. It says: treat them all as if 'their hearts are already perfect', because in fact all our God-given hearts are perfect. It's just our distorted vision, full of meaningless distinctions like friend or enemy, that causes us to suffer and to sometimes treat others less well than we would like. It does rob life of its dazzling complexity with all the various sorts of people, some one likes, some one hates and others who are ignored. It's a simple rule: love all, as the Prophet says, for 'simplicity, too, is a part of faith'.

Faris Badawi

✛ ✛ ✛

Those who return to the centre from their illness will have a deeper understanding of the needs of others.

Revd Rob Gillion

✛ ✛ ✛

A little while ago a lovely eighty-five-year-old lady from my previous parish in London came out to see me. She had a wonderful weekend here and at the airport on her return she said, 'You know, Murray, I've really enjoyed myself. Nobody in London notices a little old lady. But they do here. They look at you, how you're dressed. They're interested. It's made me feel more of a person.'

We could all do that. Be more interested in others, making them feel more of a person. Is there anything better than that?

Revd Murray Grant

✤ ✤ ✤

I watched a programme on TV recently about an exciting discovery in an ancient tomb. In among all the gold and treasures, they also found some grains of wheat.

And why are grains of wheat worth mentioning?

Well, as you can imagine, these were

special grains. Not only were they two thousand years old, but scientists managed to grow them into wheat!

On the face of it, the TV programme was about a scientific discovery of how seeds were preserved all this time.

But, for me, an even more important point was that these seeds still had the potential to grow into wheat – even after two thousand years.

The reason they hadn't grown was because they were deprived of the right environment – and a tomb filled with gold certainly wasn't the right place for the seeds to grow.

They needed soil, water and sun for their potential to be revealed.

And so it is for everything that grows in nature.

Fidelma Meehan

✣ ✣ ✣

I was talking the other day to the Salvation Army Captain in Harpenden. The Captain told me how his little daughter had complained: 'You're not listening, Mummy.'

'Yes, I am,' said her mother.

'Well, listen louder,' said the child.

Good advice for all of us, I think. Especially in these perilous times.

Major Charles King

BIOGRAPHICAL NOTES

Faris Badawi is the Administrator of the
Muslim College in London.

Rt Revd Kieran Conry is the Roman Catholic
Bishop of Arundel and Brighton.

Father Brian D'Arcy is a Passionist priest
from Ireland.

Krishna Dharma is a Vaishnava priest, author
and consultant on Hinduism.

Revd Joel Edwards is the General Director of
the Evangelical Alliance.

Revd Robert Gillion is an Anglican vicar in
Chelsea and Officer for Evangelism in the
Kensington Diocese.

Revd Murray Grant is an Anglican priest. He is Chaplain to the British Forces at NATO in Naples.

Revd Rose Hudson-Wilkin is an Anglican priest and the Vicar of Holy Trinity Dalston and All Saints Hagerston.

Commissioner Alex Hughes is the Salvation Army's Territorial Commander in the United Kingdom.

Revd Roy Jenkins is a Baptist minister living in Wales.

Major Charles King is the Editor of the Salvation Army's *Salvationist*.

Fr Wilfrid McGreal is the Prior of the Carmelite Community at Aylesford Priory.

Oliver McTernan is a writer and broadcaster.

Fidelma Meehan is Projects Co-ordinator for the Baha'is in Swindon.

Father Shaun Middleton is the Catholic Parish Priest at St Francis of Assisi Church in Pottery Lane, London.

Dharmachari Nagaraja is a member of the London Buddhist Centre.

Revd John Rackley is the Minister at Manvers Street Baptist Church, Bath.

Revd Dr Stephen C. Rettenmayer is Senior Minister of the American Church in London.

Rabbi Y.Y. Rubinstein is the Jewish Chaplain for the University of Manchester.

Revd Ruth Scott is an Anglican priest in Richmond.

Indarjit Singh is the Editor of *The Sikh Messenger*.

Rt Revd Roy Williamson is the former Anglican Bishop of Southwark.

Rt Revd Tom Wright is the Anglican Bishop of Durham.